Queen
OF Scots

CONTENTS

Designed and produced by David Salariya
Edited by Diana J. Holubowicz

Copyright © The Salariya Book Company Ltd 1994

First published in 1994 by
PAN MACMILLAN CHILDREN'S BOOKS
A division of Pan Macmillan Limited
Cavaye Place London SW10 9PG

ISBN 0-333-5944-60 (Macmillan hardback)
ISBN 0-333-3299-36 (Piccolo paperback)

A CIP catalogue record for this book is available from the British Library

Printed in Hong Kong

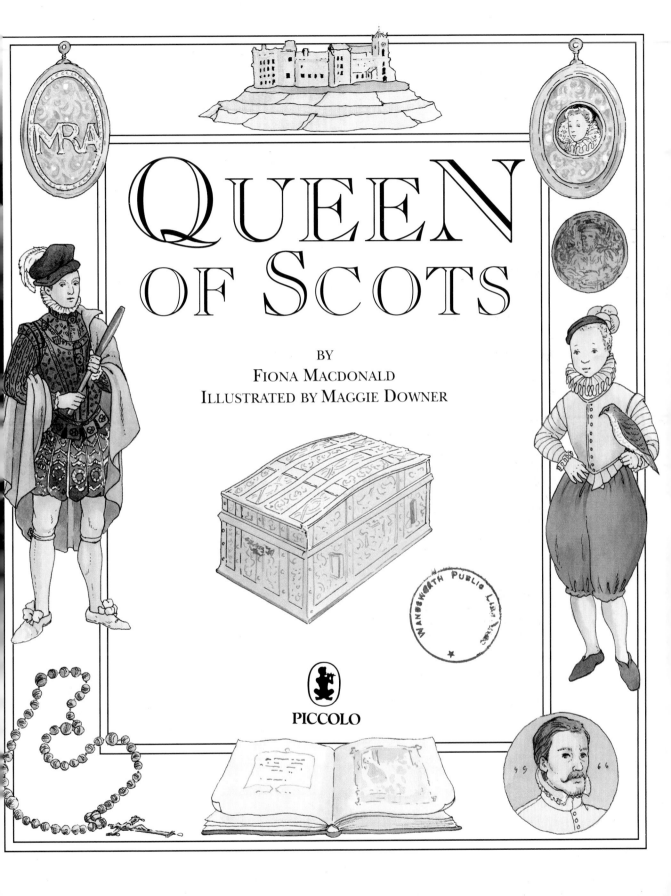

QueeN
OF SCOTS

BY
FIONA MACDONALD
ILLUSTRATED BY MAGGIE DOWNER

PICCOLO

INTRODUCTION

Mary Queen of Scots is one of the most famous women in history. She lived in the sixteenth century, over four hundred years ago. For most of her life, Europe was at war. Rival nations wanted wealth and power, but their most important reason for fighting was religion. Some countries were Catholic, others were Protestant.

Mary's Catholic beliefs meant that she was likely to be mistrusted by half of Europe, almost from the day she was born. But Mary seemed special. Even as a child, she was praised, petted and admired. Poets wrote songs about her beauty and charm. Princes liked her high spirits and lively mind. And rough Scottish nobleman fought to win her favour.

Yet Mary ended her life as a sick, miserable, lonely prisoner in a foreign land. What went wrong? Were her misfortunes her own fault, or was she the tragic victim of events she could not control? You can read Mary's story in this book.

ROYAL FAMILIES

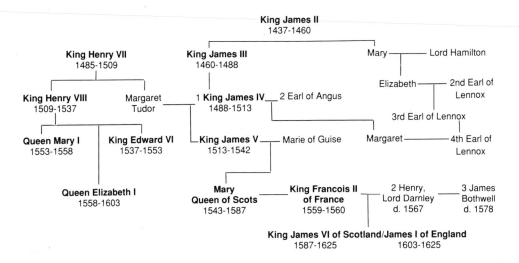

Mary was the third child of King James V of Scotland. Her mother was a French noblewoman, Marie of Guise. Mary had two elder brothers, but tragically, they both died in 1541. Now King James and Queen Marie needed an heir.

Mary was born on 8 December 1542. She was a sickly baby, and her mother became dangerously ill after giving birth. Worse still, Mary's father died just six days later. For a time, it looked as if the whole Scottish royal family would perish. But Mary and her mother survived, and Mary became Queen.

Mary was descended from the English royal family, as well as the Scots. Her great-grandfather, Henry VII, had been King of England.

Mary became Queen of Scotland because her father died without any male heirs. As you can see, Mary was also next in line to become Queen of England, if Elizabeth I left no children to inherit her crown.

In fact, Mary died before Elizabeth, but her son James, did become King of England in 1603.

People in Scotland greeted the news of Mary's birth with disappointment. They would have preferred a boy. They feared that when Mary married, her husband – probably a foreign prince – would take control of their country. They also feared that Scotland's hostile neighbour, England, would try to invade if there were no strong king to lead the Scottish army into war.

Mary was crowned Queen of Scotland on 9 September 1543, when she was only nine months old. Three noblemen carried her crown, sword and sceptre. Many nobles stayed away, because they did not think it was right for a baby girl to rule.

A 'PERFECT CHILD'

Sixteenth-century Scotland was not a peaceful place to live. King James was dead, rival nobles fought to win power, and English troops invaded. Marie of Guise was frightened. How could she keep Mary safe amid all these struggles? Marie asked France for help. She arranged a marriage between Mary and the French Crown Prince. In France, Mary would be safe, and, when she grew up, she would be the French queen.

Mary spent many weeks with her French royal friends (and their twenty six pet dogs) at the chateau (palace) of Chambord, in western France. Chambord was just one of many grand new homes built by the French king's father, King François I, in the latest style. It had over four hundred rooms, all richly decorated. On her visits to these beautiful buildings, Mary learned to enjoy elegance and luxury.

In 1548, Mary was sent to France. She was not quite six years old. She spent the next twelve years there, very happily. She shared lessons and playtime with the French royal children, including Prince François, her husband-to-be.

From their first meeting, they were friends. Mary was pretty, lively, and intelligent, and soon became a favourite with the King. He called her 'the most perfect child'.

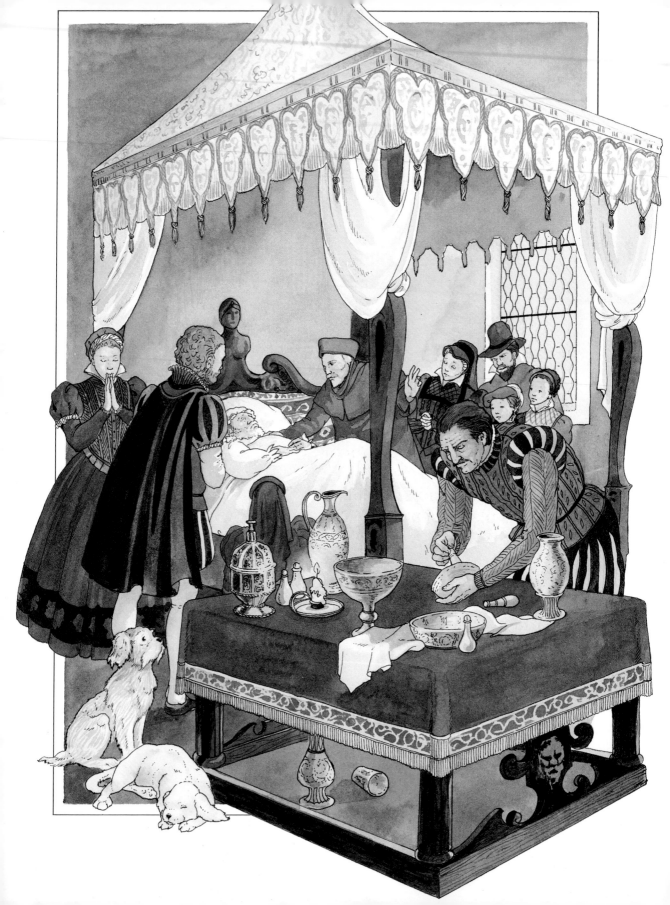

A Tragic Year

King Henri II of France was a busy man. He was a soldier, a diplomat, and a good administrator. He fought to protect the Church. He spent many hours with his children. To relax, he liked to fight mock battles, called tournaments. In July 1559, at a tournament, a stray spear pierced his eye. He soon became unconscious, and died just a few days later.

Mary was one of the chief mourners at King Henri's funeral. She had married his son, Prince François, just eighteen months before. Now Henri was dead, and François was king in his place. Mary became queen of Scotland and France.

King François was proud of Mary, his beautiful bride. And although Mary did not love her husband, she remained his loyal friend. They looked forward to many years together. But in December 1559, King François – who was never strong – died of an ear infection. Queen Mary was a widow.

The cathedral of Notre Dame in Paris, where Mary married Prince François in 1558. Mary wore a priceless jewelled crown and a white robe. This was an unusual colour for weddings in those days, but it suited Mary's fair skin, hazel eyes and red hair.

Mary's gold ring, decorated with a lion, a symbol of Scotland. On the back, Mary's initials are joined with François's, to show their friendship.

RETURN TO SCOTLAND

Fifteen fifty nine was a tragic year for Mary. Her happy life at the French court had ended. Far away in Scotland, her mother, Marie of Guise, had died. Although Mary had not seen her mother since she was five, they often wrote, and exchanged poems, books and gifts.

Mary – now aged eighteen – had to make some difficult decisions about her future. Should she stay in France and live quietly as a widow? Should she marry another foreign prince? Or should she return to her own kingdom of Scotland, and govern the country herself?

Mary chose to go to Scotland, where she hoped she could be independent. Compared with France, Scotland was cold, poor, and uncivilized. Its people were rude and rough. Royal power was threatened by ambitious nobles. Nervously, Mary left France in 1561. She was given a warm welcome by the Scottish people, but who knew what would happen next?

Parliament Decides

In 1560, the Scottish Parliament met to discuss religion. MPs had to decide whether the Scottish people should worship in the old Catholic way, or whether they should follow the teachings of the new Protestant faith.

John Knox believed all women, including Mary, were 'weak, frail, impatient, foolish creatures', not fit to rule.

Today it seems odd that religious beliefs should be laid down by law, but sixteenth-century governments knew that religious disagreements could soon lead to civil war.

Parliament favoured the Protestant faith. Members were unhappy with how the Catholic Church was run. They did not believe all its teachings. So Scotland became Protestant. Preachers like John Knox gave rousing sermons, calling on people to live good, sober lives.

The Scottish MPs had made a democratic decision. But soon they faced a problem. Mary, their queen, was a Catholic. She agreed to let people worship in a Protestant way, but she would not change her own faith. To John Knox, this was a disgrace. He told Mary that she should no longer be queen.

QUEEN OF SCOTS

Queen Elizabeth of England feared that Mary might marry a Catholic prince. At Elizabeth's court in London, royal advisors planned to persuade Mary to stay single, or only to marry if Elizabeth approved.

Now they were home, Mary, her ladies-in-waiting and servants, moved into Holyrood Palace in Edinburgh, Scotland's capital city. Like Queen Elizabeth, Mary spent much time on government business, discussing with Scottish nobles her plans to improve the economy, to calm religious tensions, and to prevent war. Mary also took advice from foreign servants she brought to Scotland with her from France. Mary's decisions were mostly sensible and fair; she wanted peace at home and abroad.

Mary spent her free time entertaining visitors. Their favourite amusements were dancing, parties, and banquets. For fun, Mary enjoyed dressing up in boys' clothes and wandering about the city after dark. John Knox and the Edinburgh citizens were scandalized. She also liked riding, hunting and archery.

Mary's independent life ended in 1565 when she made the disastrous decision to marry her cousin Henry, Lord Darnley.

MURDER

Mary had to marry, because it was her duty to have children. Scotland needed future kings and queens. Mary was young, rich and beautiful; many men would have been pleased to marry her. It is hard to see why she chose Darnley, except perhaps for political reasons. Darnley was closely related to the English royal family. Their children might therefore rule England and Scotland when Queen Elizabeth died. Darnley was handsome, but he was also drunken, greedy, and extremely foolish.

Although she was deeply shocked, Mary did not faint or run away when Riccio was attacked. As soon as they heard shouting, her loyal foreign servants hurried to protect her.

Darnley was not a good husband. He interfered in politics, spent too much of Mary's money, and was jealous. In particular, he disliked David Riccio, Mary's Italian secretary. Mary and Riccio shared a love of poetry and music, and spent long evenings together, talking, singing, and playing cards. Darnley decided that Riccio must go. He arranged for a group of Scottish nobles to rush into Mary's private rooms one night, seize Riccio, and stab him to death.

THE WICKED LORD

Prince James had a very different character from Mary, his mother. He loved books, not people, and was rather dull and boring. People called him the 'wisest fool in Christendom'.

James Hepburn, Earl of Bothwell. A copy of the only known portrait of him, painted in 1566. He was then about thirty years old.

At the time of Riccio's murder, Mary was pregnant. There were celebrations when she gave birth to a son, Prince James, in June 1566. But they were soon followed by shock and suspicion.

In 1567, the house where Darnley was staying blew up, shortly after Mary had visited it. Darnley's body was found outside – strangled. Weeks later, Mary married again. Her third husband was James Hepburn, Earl of Bothwell, a bold, brave, ruthless landowner, who was suspected of plotting Darnley's death. People were scandalized. They knew Mary hated Darnley. Had she helped to kill him so she could marry this 'wicked lord'?

The leading nobles decided to act. They put Mary in prison on Loch Leven, and chased Bothwell out of the country. In 1568, Mary, disguised as a servant, escaped and fled to England. Some Scots stayed loyal to Mary; others did not want her as their queen.

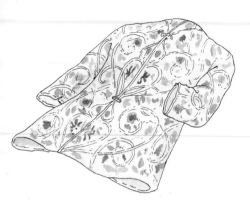

Part of a jacket embroidered by Mary during her years in captivity. Embroidered clothes were worn by wealthy men and women during the sixteenth century. Mary often decorated her embroidery with designs containing a political 'message' about her lonely captivity.

Small, elegant harp, which Mary played to entertain herself and her ladies-in-waiting.

In Captivity

Mary arrived in England dressed in dirty, borrowed clothes, and exhausted after a long, dangerous journey. She had few servants and no money. Even so, she was pleased to arrive. She had escaped from her Scottish enemies, and she believed that her cousin, Queen Elizabeth, would look after her, and help her win back her rightful place as Queen of Scots.

But Mary was mistaken. Elizabeth saw her as a rival. And English people disliked Mary's Catholic faith. They were suspicious of her friendship with England's enemy, France, and did not want to get involved in a war with Scotland. What should Elizabeth do? If she let Mary live free in England, she might plot to seize power. If she sent her back to Scotland, hostile nobles would kill her. If she let her go to France, then Mary might help French invaders. So Elizabeth kept Mary locked up, first as a 'guest' and then as a prisoner, for the next eighteen years.

Mary Must Die

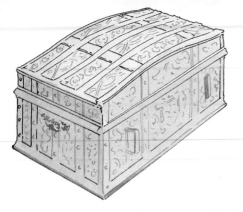

The famous silver casket, which once contained passionate letters, possibly written by Mary to Bothwell while her husband Darnley was still alive. These 'Casket Letters' disappeared four hundred years ago. Historians do not know whether they were real or fake.

Mary's beautifully-illustrated prayer book. Mary remained true to the Catholic faith all her life.

Mary's golden rosary, which she carried with her to her execution.

At first, Mary looked forward to being set free. But Scottish nobles produced letters (the 'Casket Letters'), which, they said, proved that Mary had helped to kill Darnley. Many people now believed she was guilty, and should spend the rest of her life in gaol. Even her son was taught to hate her.

Elizabeth feared that Mary would try to escape. So she moved her prison lodgings from comfortable houses to a grim castle. Mary's private letters were opened, and her visitors were watched.

English government spies discovered that Mary's friends were plotting to set her free, and that some English Catholics planned to make her queen. They warned that Mary was becoming a danger to the kingdom, and that she should be put on trial. Sadly, Elizabeth agreed. Mary was tried, and found guilty of treason. She was sentenced to death, and executed on 8 February 1587. She was forty-four years old.

TIME CHART

MARY'S LIFETIME

1542   Mary born 8 December.

1552   Mary's father, King James V of Scotland dies on 14 December.

1543   Mary is crowned Queen of Scotland.

1548   Mary goes to live in France, aged five.

1558   Mary marries Prince François of France.

1559   (June) Mary becomes Queen of France.

1559   (December) Mary's husband dies.

1561   Mary returns to Scotland.

1565   Mary marries Henry, Lord Darnley.

1566   Mary's secretary, David Riccio, is murdered.

1566   Mary's son, James, is born. Later, he becomes King James VI of Scotland and King James I of England.

1567   Mary's second husband, Henry, Lord Darnley, is murdered.

1567   Mary marries James Hepburn, Earl of Bothwell, who is suspected of plotting to kill Darnley.

1567   Angry Scottish nobles put Mary in prison.

1568   Mary escapes and flees to England. She is locked up by Queen Elizabeth.

1587   Mary is suspected of plotting against Queen Elizabeth. She is tried for treason, found guilty and executed.

EUROPE

1542 Scots army defeated by English at Solway Moss.

1558 Elizabeth I Queen of England.

1559 King Henri II of France wounded at a tournament and dies a few days later.

1559 John Knox returns to Scotland after studying Protestant teachings in Switzerland.

1559 Tobacco first appears in Europe from America.

1562 Religious wars begin in France and last until 1598.

1569 Rebellion against English troops in Northern Ireland.

1570 Turkish troops invade Eastern Europe.

1572 Dutch people rebel against Spanish rule.

1572 St Bartholemew's Day massacre in France; over 2,000 Protestants killed by Catholics.

1588 English defeat Spanish Armada (battle fleet).

REST OF THE WORLD

1545 Silver discovered in Peru, South America.

1549 First national assembly (Parliament) in Russia.

1555 Japanese pirates attack Chinese ports.

1556 Reign of Akbar the Great, ruler of the Mughal Empire in India.

1562 English ships make first slave-trading voyage between Africa and America.

1566 Turkish emperor Suleiman the Magnificent dies.

1567 Important government reforms in Japan.

1577 First around-the-world voyage, by English sailor Francis Drake.

1578 Moroccans drive Portuguese from Africa.

1580 Crisis in China: drought and famine.

1581 Russia conquers Siberia.

WORD LIST

Administrator A manager; someone who is good at planning tasks and organizing people.

Banquets Feasts.

Capital city The most important city in a country, usually where the government is based.

Captivity Being kept in prison.

Cathedral A large, important church.

Catholic A type of Christian believer. A person who follows the teachings of the Roman Catholic Church, led by the Pope in Rome. Before the 16th century, the whole of Western Europe was Catholic.

Casket A box.

Chateau The French word for a palace or stately home.

Christendom An old word, used in the past to describe Western Europe, where people were Christians.

Civil war Fighting between rival groups within a country.

Crown prince The oldest son of a king. Usually, a crown prince becomes king after his father dies.

Democratic decision A decision that is fair, because it is based on what most people think or want.

Diplomat Someone whose job it is to maintain friendships between different countries.

Ebony A precious black wood which comes from trees growing in tropical countries.

Elegance Smart style.

Executed Killed by government orders, usually after having been tried for a serious crime and found guilty.

Execution The occasion when someone is executed.

Frail Fragile.

Gaol Prison.

Heir A son or daughter who will inherit (see below) great wealth or an important position from their father, mother, or other close relation.

Inherit To receive land, money, a title or a position from your father or mother (or other close relation) after they have died.

Initials The first letter of a person's names.

Ivory A precious, smooth, creamy-white substance, made from elephant tusks. It is used in jewellery, and to decorate other small, valuable objects.

Luxury Comfort and richness.

Mourners People who attend a funeral to show their respect for a dead person and their sorrow that he or she has died.

Passionate Full of strong feelings.

Prayer Book A book containing prayers.

Protestant A type of Christian believer. In the 16th century, many scholars – and ordinary people – criticized the Catholic Church. They did not like the way it was run, and disagreed with some of its teachings. So they complained, and became known as 'Protestants', because of their protests. Soon, they left the Catholic Church and set up churches of their own.

Pierced Stuck through.

Rosary A string of beads used by Catholics to help them remember their prayers. Each bead on a rosary represents a separate prayer. Worshippers remember the correct order of prayers by slipping the rosary beads through their fingers.

Sceptre A jewelled rod, the sign of royal authority (power).

Sermon A talk on religious subjects, designed to help people lead better lives.

Strangled Killed by being choked.

Symbol A sign or badge.

Tensions Quarrels or disagreements that might lead to fighting.

Tournament A mock battle, fought for sport and entertainment.

Trial A court case, which takes place after someone is accused of a crime. Lawyers present evidence to the court, and a judge and jury use that evidence to decide whether the accused person is innocent or guilty. The trial of Mary Queen of Scots was not very fair by modern standards. She was not allowed any lawyers to help her present her case, and most of the people at her trial wanted to see her found guilty.

Treason A crime against your own country. For example, acting as a spy for an enemy land or plotting to kill your king or queen are acts of treason.

INDEX

Notes for Teachers on History in the National Curriculum

The new National Curriculum for History, which lays down a prescribed course of study for pupils aged five to sixteen, was introduced into schools in England and Wales during the autumn term 1991.

This series of books has been designed to provide background information relevant to the designated Core history Study Units for key Stage 2 (i.e., for pupils aged seven to eleven), and also to the Optional History Study Units at the same key stage level. Younger children, in particular, should find the short, simple text and largely visual presentation of information appropriate to their needs.

Queen of Scots relates in particular to Core Study Unit CSU 2 – Tudor and Stuart Times. In the words of the National Curriculum final programme of study (*History in the National Curriculum*, HMSO, March 1991, page 21):

Pupils should be introduced to key issues and events in Tudor and Stuart times. The focus should be on the way of life of people at all levels of society, and on well-documented events and personalities of the period. Reference should be made to the histories of England, Wales, Scotland and Ireland.

Pupils should be taught about:

rulers and court life:	Tudor and Stuart rulers major events… the courts of Tudor and Stuart monarchs…
religious issues:	religious changes…

All these topics are included in this book.